Title: The Simplest Way to May Money Online: Simple tips and tricks to make money online and a sure strategy to achieve financial freedom without stress.

Andrew A. Wilson

INTRODUCTION:

In the digital age, a story unfolds - one of dreams and aspirations, woven in the fabric of the World Wide Web. It's the tale of Andrew A. Wilson, a modern-day explorer in the online realm, and his quest to unveil the simplest way to make money online.

Picture a world where pixels are your canvas, and ideas, your currency. Andrew, our guide, was not a tech prodigy or a financial wizard; he was simply a person with a dream - a dream to discover the digital goldmine hidden within the vast, uncharted territories of the internet. As dawn broke on a new era, Andrew embarked on a digital journey, armed with his experiences, insights, and a burning curiosity. He had heard whispers of success stories from all corners of the globe - tales of individuals who had cracked the code to turn their internet adventures into thriving businesses.

With every click and every keystroke, Andrew navigated through the digital wilderness, learning the secrets of online income generation. He met entrepreneurs who had turned their passions into profits, affiliate marketers who had cracked the code of commissions, and e-commerce gurus who had mastered the art of online retail.

Together, they uncovered the pathways to financial freedom within the digital realm. It wasn't always easy, and there were pitfalls along the way, but Andrew's story is one of persistence and innovation. He discovered that the simplest way to make money online lay in understanding your audience, delivering value, and staying adaptable in the ever-evolving online landscape.

But Andrew's story isn't just about financial success; it's about the people he met and the lessons he learned. It's a narrative of building trust, maintaining transparency, and providing real value to those he encountered on his digital journey.

As we step into this narrative alongside Andrew A. Wilson, we are invited to explore the digital realm for ourselves. Like a story handed down from generation to generation, this is an adventure of our time, where simplicity meets prosperity, and where the internet is not just a space for information but a gateway to financial independence.

So, come and join the adventure - where the digital goldmine beckons, and where the simplest way to make money online becomes not just a story but a reality for those who dare to explore.

Chapter one:

Introduction to Online Income Opportunities:

In the ever-evolving digital landscape, the concept of making money online has transformed from a niche idea to a widespread reality. The allure of earning income through the internet is undeniable, thanks to the flexibility, convenience, and diverse opportunities it offers.

This chapter serves as an entry point to the world of online income, where we'll explore the fundamental principles and motivations behind seeking income online. We'll set the stage for the journey ahead, addressing key questions, including what online income entails, why it's an appealing option, and how to establish realistic expectations in this dynamic landscape.

As we embark on this exploration, it's essential to understand that online income opportunities span a wide spectrum, catering to various skills, interests, and goals. Whether you're seeking a full-time career or looking to supplement your existing income, the internet holds a myriad of potential pathways to financial success.

Join us as we delve into the exciting realm of online income, uncovering the possibilities and benefits it offers to those willing to explore this digital frontier.

What Is Online Income?

Online income is a broad term that encompasses the earnings generated through various activities conducted on the internet. It represents a diverse array of opportunities for individuals and businesses to make money using the digital capabilities of the online world. These opportunities have grown in popularity due to the convenience, accessibility, and global reach that the internet provides.

Online income can take many forms, and it's not limited to a specific source or method. Some common categories of online income include:

Freelancing: This involves offering your skills or services online to clients or companies. Freelancers can provide services such as writing, graphic design, web development, digital marketing, and more.

Affiliate Marketing: In affiliate marketing, individuals promote products or services and earn a commission for each sale or lead generated through their unique affiliate links.

Digital Products: Creating and selling digital products like e-books, online courses, stock photos, software, or templates.

E-commerce and Dropshipping: Setting up and operating an online store to sell physical or digital products. This can involve managing inventory or using dropshipping methods.

Blogging and Content Creation: Content creators monetize their blogs, YouTube channels, or social media platforms through various means, including advertising, sponsored content, and affiliate marketing.

Virtual Assistance: Virtual assistants provide administrative, creative, or technical support remotely to businesses and entrepreneurs.

Online Surveys and Market Research: Individuals participate in online surveys, focus groups, and market research studies, often in exchange for compensation or rewards.

Investing and Trading: Engaging in online trading and investment activities, including stock trading, cryptocurrency investments, or forex trading.

Stock Photography and Art Sales: Selling photographs, digital art, illustrations, or other creative works on stock image websites or personal platforms.

Online Consulting and Coaching: Professionals offer their expertise in areas such as business, career, or personal development through virtual consultations or coaching sessions.

Online income opportunities are attractive to many because of the potential for remote work, the ability to connect with clients or customers globally, and the flexibility they offer. It's worth noting that success in the online income space often requires a combination of skills, dedication, adaptability, and a keen understanding of the ever-evolving digital landscape.

Why make money online?

Earning money online has become an increasingly appealing option for individuals and businesses worldwide. The internet offers a wealth of opportunities for generating income, and there are several compelling reasons why people choose to pursue online earning:

Flexibility and Convenience: Online income opportunities provide a level of flexibility that is often hard to find in traditional jobs. Many online jobs and businesses allow you to work from anywhere, set your own hours, and tailor your work environment to your preferences.

Global Reach: The internet breaks down geographical barriers. You can connect with clients, customers, or employers from around the world, broadening your income potential and diversifying your opportunities.

Diverse Income Streams: The online world offers a wide range of income-generating methods. Whether you prefer freelancing, e-commerce, content creation, or investments, there is a niche or industry to suit your interests and skills.

Low Overheads: Many online income opportunities have low startup costs compared to traditional brick-and-mortar businesses. This makes it accessible to a broader range of individuals, including those with limited capital.

Accessibility: The internet is accessible to a wide demographic, and online income opportunities are often designed to be user-friendly. You can start with minimal technical expertise and learn as you go.

Supplemental Income: Online earning can be a fantastic way to supplement your existing income. It can provide an additional revenue stream to help you achieve financial goals, pay off debts, or save for the future.

Entrepreneurial Spirit: Online income opportunities cater to the entrepreneurial spirit. Many people appreciate the autonomy and creativity that come with building their online businesses.

Remote Work: The rise of remote work has made online income more accessible than ever. Whether you're a digital nomad traveling the world or working from the comfort of your home, online earning offers new career and lifestyle possibilities.

Job Security: Diversifying your income sources by earning online can enhance your financial security. It provides an added layer of protection against unexpected job loss or economic downturns.

Continuous Learning: Online income opportunities often encourage continuous learning. Whether you're developing new skills, staying updated on industry trends, or adapting to changing market conditions, online earning can be a path of personal and professional growth.

Economic Independence: Earning online can be a step toward economic independence. It allows you to take control of your financial future and create opportunities that align with your goals.

Alternative to Traditional Employment: Online earning provides an alternative to traditional employment. It's particularly attractive for those who value autonomy and want to chart their own career paths.

Passion Projects: Many people turn their hobbies and passions into income-generating opportunities online. This can be a way to do what you love and earn from it.

In summary, the allure of earning money online lies in its flexibility, global reach, and diverse income streams. It caters to a wide range of individuals, from those seeking supplemental income to entrepreneurs looking to build thriving online businesses. Whether you're exploring online earning for financial security or to pursue your passions, the internet offers a world of opportunities waiting to be explored.

CHAPTER 2

Outsourcing Your Chops, Your Pay

Outsourcing permits you to utilize your chops and spunk to separately acquire pay. You can offer administrations in brilliant fields, from composing and plan to programming and advanced promoting. It's an adaptable method for dealing with frameworks you are enthusiastic about and procure magnate based on your conditions. Find Your Attractive Chops relating your attractive chops is the initial step to fruitful outsourcing. Think about your assets, interests, and regions where you surpass. Whether it's composition, visual depiction, web improvement, or computerized promoting, your chops can come your pass to a wonderful outsourcing vocation. Independent Stages Independent stages are online trade that unite consultants and visitors needing explicit administrations. These stages act as interposers, facilitating the most common way of finding, employing, and working with consultants. Well known independent stages incorporate Upwork, Consultant, Fiverr, Toptal, and Master, among others.

Picking the right stage relies upon your chops, target visitors, and plan inclinations. Independent stages have standardized the universe of work, empowering specialists to find frameworks and visitors comprehensively, and visitors to puncture an alternate pool of gift. These stages have come basic to the ultramodern outsourcing geology, making openings for both old pros and fledglings to the independent world. raising an Independent Profile Making a convincing independent profile is essential for drawing in visitors and getting frameworks on independent stages. Then, at that point, are significant approach to raising a viable profile Proficient Photograph Utilize an unmistakable, proficient print as your profile picture. It fabricates trust and assists visitors with seeing your name. Drawing in Title Art a concise and connecting with title that features your primary chops and pizazz. This is the primary thing visitors see.

Successful Synopsis Compose a convincing rundown that presents yourself, frames your chops, and makes sense of how you can benefit visitors. Keep it brisk and centered. Definite Portfolio Show your in vogue work in your portfolio segment. Incorporate examples of previous frameworks, exhibiting your pizazz and the nature of your work. Cleaves and instruments Rundown your chops and any relevant instruments. This assists visitors with finding you while looking for explicit hacks. Work History Detail your work history, including once frameworks and visitors. accentuate your achievements and effective coordinated efforts. client Surveys Urge fulfilled visitors to leave audits on your profile. Positive surveys make believability and trust. Evaluating and Administrations effectively characterize your valuing structure and the administrations you offer. clarity assists visitors with understanding what to expect. Amazing skill Keep up with incredible skill in your correspondence, relations, and profile content. An expert location draws in visitors. Ordinary Updates Keep your profile smoothed out with your rearmost work and achievements. A functioning profile is bound to draw in visitors.

Specialty Specialization: Think about securing on a particular specialty or assiduity. Practicing can make you stand apart to visitors looking for pizazz in a specific field. raising areas of strength for a profile takes time and inconvenience, yet a speculation can pay off with additional plan openings and high level income. adjust your profile to mirror your remarkable chops and character, and don't be crazy to exhibit your accomplishments and abilities to draw in visitors who esteem your spunk. Outcome in Outsourcing Making progress in outsourcing includes a blend of elements and techniques.

Then, at that point, is a guide to assist you with flourishing in the outsourcing scene Expertise Improvement Ceaselessly update and extend your range of abilities. Keeping awake to-date with assiduity patterns and obtaining new cleaves will make you more enticing to visitors. Statistical surveying Figure out the interest for your administrations and recognize beneficial specialties. Research the opposition and client needs to find your exceptional selling focuses. Powerful Systems administration figure serious areas of strength for an organization. Interface with different specialists, assiduity experts, and certain visitors. Systems administration can prompt references and coordinated efforts.

Outstanding Portfolio : Maintain an emotional portfolio that showcases your stylish work. Make sure it aligns with your niche and customer prospects.

Pricing Strategy: Determine your pricing strategy grounded on your chops, request rates, and design complexity. Be competitive but insure you're compensated fairly.

Time Management: Efficiently manage your time to meet design deadlines and balance multiple guests. Consider time-shadowing tools to stay systematized.

Clear Communication: Develop strong communication chops. Be clear in your dispatches, hear to customer requirements, and ask questions when necessary.

Customer connections: Cultivate positive customer connections. Address enterprises instantly, be professional, and exceed prospects to make a good character.

Harmonious Marketing: Promote your services constantly. Use social media, professional websites, and online biographies to showcase your moxie.

Specialization: Consider specializing in a niche or assiduity. Specialization can set you piecemeal and allow you to charge advanced rates.

Legal and fiscal operation : Handle legal and fiscal aspects responsibly. insure you have contracts in place, track income and charges, and set away finances for levies.

Literacy and adaption: Stay adaptable and open to literacy. The freelance geography evolves, so being flexible and eager to grow is essential.

Positive Mindset: Maintain a positive station. Freelancing can have its challenges, but a positive mindset can help you overcome obstacles and persist.

Tone- Care: Prioritize tone- care and work-life balance. Collapse can hamper your success, so take breaks and insure your well-being.

Seek Feedback: Request feedback from guests to identify areas for enhancement. Formative review can help you grow.

Diversify Income: Consider diversifying your income sources. This can reduce threat and produce stability in your freelancing career.

Invest in Tools: Invest in the right tools and software to enhance your productivity. Tools for design operation, invoicing, and communication can streamline your work.

Online Presence: Maintain a strong online presence. Regularly modernize your biographies on freelancing platforms and other online channels.

Financial Planning: Save for the future. produce an exigency fund and plan for withdrawal and unanticipated fiscal challenges.

Continual literacy Keep literacy: Attend courses, webinars, and shops to stay current in your field.

Freelancing success isn't guaranteed overnight, but with fidelity, skill development, and strategic planning, you can make a thriving freelancing career that offers both particular and fiscal prices.

Chapter 3

Affiliate Marketing Promote and Earn

This marketing is an important way to earn income by promoting products or services. The following are how to succeed in chapter marketing

Elect Your Niche: Choose a niche you are passionate about or knowledgeable in, as it'll make promoting products more authentic.

Research Affiliate: Programs Find estimable chapter programs or networks that offer products related to your niche. Consider factors like commission rates and cookie durations.

Content Creation: Produce precious content, similar as blog posts, reviews, or vids, that naturally incorporate chapter product recommendations.

Transparent Recommendations: Be transparent with your followership about your chapter connections. expose your use of chapter links to make trust.

Keyword Research: Optimize your content for applicable keywords to ameliorate hunt machine rankings and attract organic business.

Promotion: Promote your content through colorful channels, including social media, dispatch marketing, and SEO, to expand your reach.

Track transformations: Use tracking tools handed by chapter programs to cover transformations and commissions.

Make an Dispatch List: Grow an dispatch list to nurture connections with your followership and promote chapter products effectively.

Nonstop Optimization: Regularly assess the performance of your chapter elevations and make adaptations to ameliorate results.

Diversify Products: Promote a variety of products to reduce reliance on a single source of income.

This marketing success hinges on furnishing value to your followership and effectively promoting products that align with their interests and requirements.

Understanding Affiliate Marketing

This marketing is a performance- grounded marketing strategy where individualities, known as cells or publishers, promote products or services on behalf of businesses, known as merchandisers or advertisers. This is how it works:

Parties Involved
chapter/ Publisher: The individual or reality promoting the product.

Merchant/ Advertiser: The business that owns the product or service being promoted.

Consumer: The end stoner who makes a purchase through the chapter's promotional sweats

Affiliate's Role: Affiliates choose products or services to promote grounded on their niche or target followership. They admit unique chapter links or tracking canons from the trafficker to track their referrals.

Promotion styles: Affiliates use colorful marketing channels like websites, blogs, social media, dispatch, or YouTube to promote the products. They produce content that features these products and includes their chapter links.

Earning Commissions: When a consumer clicks on the chapter's unique link and makes a purchase, the chapter earns a commission, which is a chance of the trade's value. Commissions vary grounded on the chapter program and product.

Tracking and eyefuls: Chapter links contain tracking eyefuls that record the stoner's exertion. These eyefuls generally have a predefined duration during which the chapter can earn a commission if the stoner makes a purchase. **Affiliate Networks:** Numerous merchandisers use chapter networks to manage their chapter programs.

These networks give a centralized platform where cells can find products to promote and track their earnings.

Translucency and Disclosure: Moral part publicists uncover their branch-off associations with their group to stay aware of straightforwardness and trust.

Benefits for Auxiliaries:

Auxiliaries can procure commissions without making their own things.They have versatility in getting things that line with their claim to fame or group. Branch-off advancing can turn out inert income as additional laid out satisfied continues to create bargains.

Benefits for Merchants: Merchants can grow their endeavor and tap into the publicizing attempts of accomplices. They pay commissions when arrangements occur, making it a down to earth.

Displaying method: Branch-off displaying can help with growing brand detectable quality and legitimacy.Accomplice displaying is a commonly helpful system that helps the two individuals and merchants. For branch-offs, it offers a strategy for adjusting their web based presence, while dealers gain extra advancing resources. Nevertheless, result in part exhibiting requires quality substance, a guaranteed understanding of the ideal vested party, and moral headway practices.

Picking a Valuable Claim to fame

Picking a useful specialty is an essential push toward part exhibiting. To do this:

Energy and Data: Select a specialty you are fiery about or have expertise in. This simplifies it to make significant substance.

Measurable reviewing: Exploration the interest and challenge inside reasonable claims to fame. A congruity among demand and reasonable competition is perfect.

Evergreen as opposed to Moving: Consider whether your specialty should be evergreen (unsurprising interest) or moving (temporary popularity).

Things and Accomplice Tasks: Assurance there are critical things and partner projects available in your picked strength.

Swarm Charm: Your specialty should agree with the interests and needs of your vested party.

Transformation Potential: Overview the potential for making pay through branch-off things or organizations inside the strength.

Picking a useful specialty incorporates: Finding a congruity between your tendencies, market revenue, and pay potential. A decision can on a very basic level impact your auxiliary advancing success.Promoting Part Things

Propelling Partner Things: Truly propelling auxiliary things requires a fundamental technique. Here are key stages:

Make Quality Substance: Cultivate extraordinary substance that teaches, enlightens, or draws in your group. This content can take various designs, for instance, blog sections, accounts, reviews, or electronic amusement posts.

Importance: Assurance the auxiliary things you advance line up with your substance and group's tendencies. The more appropriate the things, the higher the chance of progress.

Use Alluring Language: Workmanship persuading and strong copy to depict the benefits of the partner things. Include how they tackle issues or address issues.

Reliability and Straightforwardness: Be clear about your auxiliary associations. Uncover that you could get a commission if clients make a purchase through your associations. Validity develops trust.

Wellspring of motivation: Engage movement by including clear and captivating ideas to make a move (CTAs) in your substance. These can be phrases like "Figure out more," "Get everything moving," or "Buy now."

Impact Web composition improvement: Update your substance for web search instruments by using appropriate expressions. This can help with attracting regular busy time gridlock and addition your accomplice bargains.

Visuals: Use extraordinary pictures, accounts, or plans to update your substance and show the partner things as a matter of fact.

A/B Testing: Assessment with different restricted time techniques and measure their suitability. A/B testing can help you with refining your procedure.

Develop Trust: Set out a strong groundwork for yourself as a specialist in your strength. The more trust you work with your group, the more plausible they are to follow your ideas.

Extend Headway Channels: Utilize different advancing channels, including virtual diversion, email exhibiting, and notices, to contact a greater group.

Track Execution: Utilize following instruments given by part tasks to screen your presentation. This helps you with understanding what's working and what needs change.

Steady Smoothing out: Reliably assess the introduction of your part progressions and make changes considering data and analysis.

Successful headway of part things is a concordance between offering an advantage to your group and securing commissions. Your substance should resonate with your vested party and address their necessities, making the part things a steady and reasonable solution for them.

Enhancing Commissions in Partner Promoting

To increase your auxiliary exhibiting rewards, follow these procedures:

Pick Worthwhile Tasks: Select auxiliary ventures with liberal commission structures. A couple of undertakings offer higher commissions or layered rates for top performers.

Target High-Worth Things: Advance things or organizations with more noteworthy expense places, as they can achieve extra immense commissions with each arrangement.

Decisively pitch and Upsell: Urge clients to purchase related or complementary things to fabricate the normal solicitation regard and, in this way, your rewards.

Create Persuading Reviews: Specialty through and through and captivating thing overviews that offer some motivating force and engage changes. Include the upsides of the things and address probably stresses.

Impact Incidental Headways: Exploit events and extraordinary occasions by accommodating your progressions to intermittent interest. Various buyers are more prepared to make purchases during such events.

Use Email Exhibiting: Build and keep an email once-over to help leads and lift part things clearly to your endorsers. Part your overview for extra assigned headways.

Content Progression: Continually redesign your substance for web search apparatuses to attract normal busy time gridlock.

High-situating substance can provoke more auxiliary arrangements.

Cutoff points and Coupons: Offer select cutoff points or coupons to your group. This can dazzle them to make purchases through your partner associations.

Attract with Your Group: Develop a sensation of neighborhood attract with your group through comments, online diversion, and messages. Building an unflinching following can incite higher change rates.

Advance Limited Time Offers: Advance things with confined time offers, making a need to get going that urges clients to take a brief action.

Advance Confined Time Offers: Advance things with limited time offers, making a need to hurry up that urges clients to take a brief action.

Paid Publicizing: Consider Exercising paid promoting, analogous to pay- per- click(PPC) drives, to concentrate on a particular crowd and direct people to your offshoot offers.

 Offshoot Challenges Take part in associate challenges eased by systems or associations. A many proposition redundant motivators and prizes for top impersonators.

 Track and anatomize Information: Routinely break down your donation information to comprehend what works and what doesn't. use this data to settle on information driven choices.

Enhance Partner systems: Advance particulars from different attachment systems to lessen reliance on a solitary kind of profit.

Remain Informed: Keep yourself refreshed on assiduity patterns and changes in associate systems or particulars. Acclimate to showcase movements to keep up with ideal prosecution.

Expanding commissions in member showcasing requires a blend of crucial advancement, relationship fabricating, and remaining informed about request rudiments. By reliably offering some benefit to your crowd and streamlining your strategies, you can expand your offshoot profit after some time.

CHAPTER 4

Making and Dealing Motorized particulars

Motorized particulars are immaterial wares or content that are circulated electronically. They incorporate effects like digital books, online courses, programming, music, recordings, and that is just the morning. Then are central issues about motorized particulars multifariousness Motorized particulars come in different structures, from instructional substance like digital books and courses to diversion content like music and videotape.

Moment Conveyance: They can be downloaded or gotten to online ensuing steal, offering accommodation to guests.

Rigidity: Advanced particulars can be reproduced and circulated to a measureless number of purchasers without the demand for factual creation.

Worldwide Reach: They can be vended and gotten to by guests around the world, making them open to an extensive crowd.

Lower Charges: Motorized item makers constantly have lower creation and rotation costs varied with factual wares. Well known Types Normal motorized particulars incorporate digital books, computer games, advanced artificer, online courses, and programming operations. adaption Makers can acclimatize motorized particulars through one- time deals, enrollments , or permitting arrangements.

Copyright Insurance: Advanced particulars might be shielded by brand to forestall unapproved dissipation or use.

The motorized item request keeps on developing, offering precious open doors for makers to communicate a worldwide crowd and produce pay through different vehicle ways.

Content Creation figure

Content creation is the system involved with producing important and applicable data or media to draw in and illuminate a group of people. This explains the Reason Content creation fills different requirements, including training, diversion, advertising, and correspondence.

Types: Content comes in different structures, like composed papers, recordings, filmland, webcasts, infographics, and that is just the morning. Crowd Driven feasible substance is custom- made to the musts and interests of the ideal interest group. Stages Content can be distributed on spots, web- grounded entertainment, web journals, web recordings, YouTube, and different motorized channels. Quality Matters Great substance is well-informed, instructional, drawing in, and constantly takes care of an issue or resolves an inquiry.

Website design improvement For online substance, point enhancement(Web optimization) strategies are employed to further develop perceivability in web hunt tool results. Thickness constantly making and participating substance helps construct and keep a crowd of people.

Content creation is a central part of internet showcasing, marking, and correspondence. It's employed by people, associations, and associations to affiliate with their ideal interest groups and pass on dispatches really.

Dealing On the web figure

Dealing on the web includes offering particulars or administrations through advanced channels. Central issues:

Web grounded business Internet selling incorporates online business stages, your point, or stranger commercial centers like Amazon and eBay. Worldwide Reach Internet selling permits entrance to a worldwide customer base, extending request precious open doors.

Investiture Handling: Secure investiture entries are employed for dealing with exchanges and guaranteeing customer information security.

Transportation and vehicle complete delivery and vehicle strategies are abecedarian for consumer fidelity.

Promoting Online dealers use advanced advertising ways, as Website optimization, virtual entertainment, and paid announcements, to draw in and connect with guests. Customer backing Giving inconceivable customer support is significant for online dealers to fabricate trust and trustability.

contest The web- grounded request is Machiavellian, awaiting dealers to separate their particulars and proposition new worth.

Web grounded immolation has changed conventional retail and keeps on developing, offering business visionaries and associations implicit chances to communicate an extensive internet grounded crowd.

Automated sources of income figure

Recurring, automated profit is cash acquired with negligible dynamic exertion. Central issues

Types Recreating, automated profit can crop out of enterprises, land, elevations, online associations, or gains.

Confined donation It requires lower everyday consideration varied with dynamic pay sources like a customary work.

Independence from the rat race structure recreating sources of income can prompt financial security and the eventuality for all the more available energy.

Expansion: Making various automated sources of income can lessen chance and improve monetary dependability.

Automated revenue offers monetary adaptability and the chance of creating cash while you rest or seek after different interests.

Chapter 5

Contributing to a blog and Content Creation

Contributing to a blog is a well known method for sharing data, sentiments, and mastery on the web. Here are the nuts and bolts:

Content Creation: Bloggers make articles or posts on a particular theme or specialty.

Stage: Pick a writing for a blog stage like WordPress, Blogger, or Medium to distribute your substance.

Space and Facilitating: A few bloggers settle on a self-facilitated blog with their own area, while others utilize free subdomains.

Crowd: Characterize your ideal interest group and make content that requests to them.

Consistency: Consistently distribute new happy to connect with your crowd and keep up with their advantage.

Advancement: Advance your blog through web-based entertainment, Search engine optimization, and other advertising methodologies.

Intuitiveness: Empower remarks and input from your perusers to construct a local area.

Adaptation: You can bring in cash through publishing content to a blog with strategies like promotions, partner showcasing, or selling items/administrations.

Writing for a blog is a flexible and inventive method for sharing your contemplations, skill, and interests with a worldwide crowd.

Adapting Your Websites

Adapting your blog can transform your energy into a kind of revenue. Key systems include:

Promotions: Show promotions from advertisement networks like Google AdSense or work with supports.

Partner Showcasing: Advance items and procure a commission for every deal made through your subsidiary connections.

Supported Content: Cooperate with brands for supported posts or item surveys.

Sell Items/Administrations: Make and sell your own digital books, courses, product, or administrations.

Enrollment/Memberships: Offer premium substance to endorsers for a common expense.

Gifts: Permit perusers to help your blog intentionally through gifts.

Email Advertising: Assemble an email rundown and use it for offshoot advancements, item dispatches, or direct deals.

Outsourcing: Grandstand your ability to draw in independent clients in your specialty.

Adapting your blog takes time, yet with a devoted crowd and excellent substance, it can turn into a feasible pay source.

Assembling and Drawing in Your Crowd

Developing and drawing in your blog's crowd is fundamental for its prosperity. Here are key techniques:

Quality Substance: Make significant, well-informed, and drawing in satisfied that resounds with your interest group.

Consistency: Distribute content consistently to make your crowd want more and more.

Web optimization: Improve your substance for web crawlers to draw in natural rush hour gridlock.

Web-based Entertainment: Advance your blog on friendly stages to extend your span and interface with your crowd.

Email Promoting: Assemble an email rundown to sustain associations with your perusers and keep them refreshed.

Commitment: Answer remarks and draw in with your perusers to encourage a feeling of local area.

Organizing: Interface with different bloggers and team up on ventures to grow your scope.

Investigation: Use information to as needs be grasp your crowd's inclinations and designer your substance.

By zeroing in on these techniques, you can construct a dependable and connected with readership, which is fundamental for the drawn out progress of your blog.

CONCLUSION

Bringing in cash online offers a universe of conceivable outcomes, however it's not generally so basic as it might appear. It requires commitment, exertion, and a thoroughly examined methodology. Whether it's through outsourcing, partner promoting, web based business, or some other strategy, achievement frequently relies on grasping your interest group, offering some benefit, and remaining versatile in the always developing advanced scene.

Chasing after web-based pay, recall that there's nobody size-fits-all methodology. What works for one individual probably won't work for another. It's critical to investigate different techniques, examine your abilities, interests, and market patterns, and persistently refine your way to deal with track down the least difficult method for bringing in cash online that lines up with your objectives and aspirations.

In your web-based adventures, focus on moral practices, keep up with straightforwardness, and endeavor to offer certifiable benefit to your crowd or clients. Progress in bringing in cash online frequently remains closely connected with building trust and conveying quality.

Eventually, the least difficult method for bringing in cash online is the one that adjusts best to your remarkable abilities, interests, and conditions. It may not generally be straightforward practically speaking, but rather with tirelessness and a promise to learning and adjusting, online pay valuable open doors can prompt monetary freedom and a satisfying web-based profession.

www.ingramcontent.com/pod-product-compliance
Lightning Source LLC
Chambersburg PA
CBHW062253290526
45794CB00006B/2536